Winter Warmers

Winter Warmers

Love Food™ is an imprint of Parragon Books Ltd

Parragon
Queen Street House
4 Queen Street
Bath BA1 1HE, UK

ISBN 978-1-4075-0266-3

Printed in China

Photography by Mike Cooper
Home Economy by Sumi Glass and Lincoln Jefferson
Cover and internal design by Mark Cavanagh
Introduction by Linda Doeser

Notes for the reader

• This book uses metric and imperial measurements. Follow the same units of measurement throughout; do not mix imperial and metric.
• All spoon measurements are level: teaspoons are assumed to be 5 ml and tablespoons are assumed to be 15 ml.
• Unless otherwise stated, milk is assumed to be low fat and eggs are medium-size. The times given are an approximate guide only.
• Some recipes contain nuts. If you are allergic to nuts you should avoid using them and any products containing nuts. Recipes using raw or very lightly cooked eggs should be avoided by infants, the elderly, pregnant women, convalescents and anyone suffering from illness.

CONTENTS

Introduction

When the evenings are drawing in and it is getting cold outside, we really learn to value the cosy comforts of home and chief among these is a warming and satisfying meal. Once at home with the curtains drawn against the elements and, if we are lucky, a fire blazing in the hearth, we are less inclined to go out again and brave unpleasant weather so home-cooking rises up our list of priorities. Appetites tend to be much heartier in the winter months and fortifying soups, stews and casseroles make a welcome return to the family menu. What could be more comforting on a cold and wet evening or a grey and dreary lunchtime than a substantial home-made soup? What is more delightful than returning home from a brisk walk through crisp snow to the appetizing aroma of a gently bubbling stew?

In this book you will find plenty of slowly cooked recipes for when you have time to allow an assortment of ingredients to simmer together slowly until their flavours have blended – these would be perfect for the weekends and holidays. For extra convenience, many of these dishes can also be made ahead and reheated when needed – in fact, this will only serve to enhance the delicious flavours. However,

since family suppers often need to be prepared and cooked quickly, you will also find included lots of equally cheering, filling and scrumptious dishes that take less time to cook. Speedy hob suppers that feature warming spices – from chilli to saffron – are the perfect choice for a miserable winter evening.

The recipes in this book have been inspired by dishes from around the world. The sheer variety of dishes – all of them packed with flavour – guarantees that there is sure to be something to suit all tastes and occasions. The book is divided into five easy-reference chapters starting with meal-in-a-bowl soups and then featuring meat, poultry, fish and seafood, and vegetables respectively, so you will never be short of ideas, however long the winter drags on! As an added bonus, these are all one-pot dishes, which certainly makes clearing up afterwards less of a chore, especially as many can be cooked and served in the same dish. Less energy is used to cook them, making a useful saving on the family budget.

In fact, you may even enjoy this superb collection of diverse, flavoursome and hearty winter warmers so much that you will be disappointed when spring finally arrives!

1

Meal-in-a-Bowl Soups

Home-made soup is the ultimate comfort food and the perfect choice for a weekend lunch. Serve it with crusty bread or rolls and, perhaps, some cheese and you will have a filling, well-balanced meal for all the family. There are some very good-quality bouillon powders and ready-made stocks available nowadays, so it need not be a chore to rustle up a brimming bowl of soup, broth or chowder.

Chunky Minestrone

Heat the oil in a large saucepan. Add the garlic, onions and Parma ham and cook over a medium heat, stirring, for 3 minutes, until slightly softened. Add the red and orange peppers and the chopped tomatoes and cook for a further 2 minutes, stirring. Stir in the stock, then add the celery. Drain and add the borlotti beans along with the cabbage, peas and parsley. Season with salt and pepper. Bring to the boil, then lower the heat and simmer for 30 minutes.

Add the vermicelli to the pan. Cook for a further 10–12 minutes, or according to the instructions on the packet. Remove from the heat and ladle into serving bowls. Garnish with freshly grated Parmesan and serve with fresh crusty bread.

SERVES 4

2 tbsp olive oil

2 garlic cloves, chopped

2 red onions, chopped

75 g/2^3/$_4$ oz Parma ham, sliced

1 red pepper, deseeded and chopped

1 orange pepper, deseeded and chopped

400 g/14 oz canned chopped tomatoes

1 litre/1^3/$_4$ pints vegetable stock

1 celery stick, trimmed and sliced

400 g/14 oz canned borlotti beans

100 g/3^1/$_2$ oz green leafy cabbage, shredded

75 g/2^3/$_4$ oz frozen peas, defrosted

1 tbsp chopped fresh parsley

salt and pepper

75 g/2^3/$_4$ oz dried vermicelli

freshly grated Parmesan cheese, to garnish

fresh crusty bread, to serve

French Onion Soup

Thinly slice the onions. Heat the olive oil in a large, heavy-based saucepan, then add the onions and cook, stirring occasionally, for 10 minutes, until they are just beginning to brown. Stir in the chopped garlic, sugar and thyme, then reduce the heat and cook, stirring occasionally, for 30 minutes, or until the onions are golden brown.

Sprinkle in the flour and cook, stirring for 1–2 minutes. Stir in the wine. Gradually stir in the stock and bring to the boil, skimming off any scum that rises to the surface, then reduce the heat and simmer for 45 minutes. Meanwhile, preheat the grill to medium. Toast the bread on both sides under the grill. Rub the toast with the garlic clove.

Ladle the soup into 6 flameproof bowls set on a baking sheet. Float a piece of toast in each bowl and divide the grated cheese among them. Place under the preheated grill for 2–3 minutes, or until the cheese has just melted. Garnish with thyme and serve.

SERVES 6

675 g/1 lb 8 oz onions

3 tbsp olive oil

4 garlic cloves, 3 chopped and 1 peeled but kept whole

1 tsp sugar

2 tsp chopped fresh thyme

2 tbsp plain flour

125 ml/4 fl oz dry white wine

2 litres/$3^1/_2$ pints vegetable stock

6 slices of French bread

300 g/$10^1/_2$ oz Gruyère cheese, grated

fresh thyme sprigs, to garnish

Mexican-style Beef & Rice Soup

Heat half the oil in a large saucepan over a medium–high heat. Add the meat in one layer and cook until well browned, turning to colour all sides. Using a slotted spoon, transfer the meat to a plate. Drain off the oil and wipe out the pan with kitchen paper.

Heat the remaining oil in the saucepan over a medium heat. Add the onion, cover and cook for about 3 minutes, stirring occasionally, until just softened. Add the green pepper, chilli, garlic and carrot, and continue cooking, covered, for 3 minutes.

Add the coriander, cumin, cinnamon, oregano, bay leaf and orange rind. Stir in the tomatoes and stock, along with the beef and wine. Bring almost to the boil and when the mixture begins to bubble, reduce the heat to low. Cover and simmer gently, stirring occasionally, for about 1 hour until the meat is tender.

Stir in the rice, raisins and chocolate, and continue cooking, stirring occasionally, for about 30 minutes until the rice is tender.

Ladle into warmed bowls and serve, garnished with coriander.

SERVES 4

3 tbsp olive oil

500 g/1 lb 2 oz boneless stewing beef, cut into 2.5-cm/1-inch pieces

1 onion, finely chopped

1 green pepper, cored, deseeded and finely chopped

1 small fresh red chilli, deseeded and finely chopped

2 garlic cloves, finely chopped

1 carrot, finely chopped

$1/4$ tsp ground coriander

$1/4$ tsp ground cumin

$1/8$ tsp ground cinnamon

$1/4$ tsp dried oregano

1 bay leaf

grated rind of $1/2$ orange

400 g/14 oz canned chopped tomatoes

1.2 litres/2 pints beef stock

150 ml/5 fl oz red wine

50 g/$1^3/4$ oz long-grain white rice

25 g/1 oz/3 tbsp raisins

15 g/$1/2$ oz plain chocolate, melted

chopped fresh coriander, to garnish

Scotch Broth

Cut the meat into small pieces, removing as much fat as possible. Put into a large saucepan and cover with the water. Bring to the boil over a medium heat and skim off any scum that appears.

Add the pearl barley, reduce the heat and cook gently, covered, for 1 hour.

Add the garlic and prepared vegetables and season well with salt and pepper. Continue to cook for a further hour. Remove from the heat and allow to cool slightly.

Remove the meat from the saucepan using a slotted spoon and strip the meat from the bones. Discard the bones and any fat or gristle. Place the meat back in the saucepan and leave to cool thoroughly, then refrigerate overnight.

Scrape the solidified fat off the surface of the soup. Reheat, season with salt and pepper to taste and serve piping hot, garnished with the parsley scattered over the top.

SERVES 6–8

700 g/1 lb 9 oz neck of lamb

1.7 litres/3 pints water

55 g/2 oz pearl barley

1 garlic clove, finely chopped

2 onions, chopped

3 small turnips, diced

3 carrots, peeled and thinly sliced

2 celery sticks, sliced

2 leeks, sliced

salt and pepper

2 tbsp chopped fresh parsley,
   to garnish

Chorizo & Red Kidney Bean Soup

Heat the oil in a large saucepan. Add the garlic and onions and cook over a medium heat, stirring, for 3 minutes, until slightly softened. Add the red pepper and cook for a further 3 minutes, stirring. In a bowl, mix the cornflour with enough stock to make a smooth paste and stir it into the pan. Cook, stirring, for 2 minutes. Stir in the remaining stock, then add the potatoes and season with salt and pepper. Bring to the boil, then lower the heat and simmer for 25 minutes, until the vegetables are tender.

Add the chorizo, courgettes and kidney beans to the pan. Cook for 10 minutes, then stir in the cream and cook for a further 5 minutes. Remove from the heat and ladle into serving bowls. Serve with slices of fresh bread.

SERVES 4

2 tbsp olive oil

2 garlic cloves, chopped

2 red onions, chopped

1 red pepper, deseeded and
  chopped

2 tbsp cornflour

1 litre/$1^3/_4$ pints vegetable stock

450 g/1 lb potatoes, peeled, halved
  and sliced

salt and pepper

150 g/$5^1/_2$ oz chorizo, sliced

2 courgettes, trimmed and sliced

200 g/7 oz canned red kidney
  beans, drained

125 ml/4 fl oz double cream

thick slices of fresh bread, to serve

Chicken Gumbo Soup

Heat the oil in a large heavy-based saucepan over a medium–low heat and stir in the flour. Cook for about 15 minutes, stirring occasionally, until the mixture is a rich golden brown.

Add the onion, green pepper and celery and continue cooking for about 10 minutes until the onion softens.

Slowly pour in the stock and bring to the boil, stirring well and scraping the bottom of the pan to mix in the flour. Remove the pan from the heat.

Add the tomatoes and garlic. Stir in the okra and rice and season. Reduce the heat, cover and simmer for 20 minutes, or until the okra is tender.

Add the chicken and sausage and continue simmering for about 10 minutes. Taste and adjust the seasoning, if necessary, and ladle into warm bowls to serve.

SERVES 6

2 tbsp olive oil

4 tbsp plain flour

1 onion, finely chopped

1 small green pepper, cored, deseeded and finely chopped

1 stalk celery, finely chopped

1.2 litres/2 pints chicken stock

400 g/14 oz can chopped tomatoes in juice

3 garlic cloves, finely chopped or crushed

125 g/$4^{1}/_{2}$ oz okra, stems removed, cut into 5-mm/$^{1}/_{4}$-inch slices

50 g/$1^{3}/_{4}$ oz white rice

200 g/7 oz cooked chicken, cubed

115 g/4 oz cooked garlic sausage, sliced or cubed

Turkey & Lentil Soup

Heat the oil in a large saucepan. Add the garlic and onion and cook over a medium heat, stirring, for 3 minutes, until slightly softened. Add the mushrooms, red pepper and tomatoes and cook for a further 5 minutes, stirring. Pour in the stock and red wine, then add the cauliflower, carrot and red lentils. Season with salt and pepper. Bring to the boil, then lower the heat and simmer the soup gently for 25 minutes, until the vegetables are tender and cooked through.

Add the turkey and courgette to the pan and cook for 10 minutes. Stir in the shredded basil and cook for a further 5 minutes, then remove from the heat and ladle into serving bowls. Garnish with basil leaves and serve with fresh crusty bread.

SERVES 4

1 tbsp olive oil

1 garlic clove, chopped

1 large onion, chopped

200 g/7 oz mushrooms, sliced

1 red pepper, deseeded and chopped

6 tomatoes, skinned, deseeded and chopped

1.2 litre/2 pints chicken stock

150 ml/5 fl oz red wine

85 g/3 oz cauliflower florets

1 carrot, peeled and chopped

200 g/7 oz red lentils

salt and pepper

350 g/12 oz cooked turkey meat, chopped

1 courgette, trimmed and chopped

1 tbsp shredded fresh basil

basil leaves, to garnish

thick slices of fresh crusty bread, to serve

Clam & Corn Chowder

Melt the butter in a large saucepan over a medium–low heat. Add the onion and carrot and cook for 3–4 minutes, stirring frequently, until the onion is softened. Stir in the flour and continue cooking for 2 minutes.

Slowly add about half the stock and stir well, scraping the bottom of the pan to mix in the flour. Pour in the remaining stock and the water and bring just to the boil, stirring.

Add the potatoes, sweetcorn and milk and stir to combine. Reduce the heat and simmer gently, partially covered, for about 20 minutes, stirring occasionally, until all the vegetables are tender.

Chop the clams, if large. Stir in the clams and continue cooking for about 5 minutes until heated through. Taste and adjust the seasoning, if needed.

Ladle the soup into bowls and serve, sprinkled with parsley.

SERVES 4

4 tsp butter

1 large onion, finely chopped

1 small carrot, finely diced

3 tbsp plain flour

300 ml/10 fl oz fish stock

200 ml/7 fl oz water

450 g/1 lb potatoes, diced

125 g/4 oz cooked or defrosted frozen sweetcorn

450 ml/16 fl oz full-fat milk

280 g/10 oz canned clams, drained and rinsed

salt and pepper

chopped fresh parsley, to garnish

2

Meat Feasts

This chapter features slow-cooked, succulent stews and casseroles that simply melt deliciously in the mouth, whether beef, lamb or pork. They have the additional benefit of being extremely economical because they use the less expensive cuts of meat. However, quicker-cooked but just as tasty dishes, such as a Sausage & Bean Casserole and Red Curry Pork with Peppers, are also included – perfect for a midweek supper.

Beef in Beer with Herb Dumplings

Preheat the oven to 160°C/325°F/Gas Mark 3. Heat the oil in a flameproof casserole. Add the onions and carrots and cook over a low heat, stirring occasionally, for 5 minutes, or until the onions are softened. Meanwhile, place the flour in a polythene bag and season with salt and pepper. Add the stewing steak to the bag, tie the top and shake well to coat. Do this in batches, if necessary.

Remove the vegetables from the casserole with a slotted spoon and reserve. Add the stewing steak to the casserole, in batches, and cook, stirring frequently, until browned all over. Return all the meat and the onions and carrots to the casserole and sprinkle in any remaining seasoned flour. Pour in the stout and add the sugar, bay leaves and thyme. Bring to the boil, cover and transfer to the preheated oven to bake for 1¾ hours.

To make the herb dumplings, sift the flour and salt into a bowl. Stir in the suet and parsley and add enough of the water to make a soft dough. Shape into small balls between the palms of your hands. Add to the casserole and return to the oven for 30 minutes. Remove and discard the bay leaves. Serve immediately, sprinkled with chopped parsley.

SERVES 6

2 tbsp sunflower oil

2 large onions, thinly sliced

8 carrots, sliced

4 tbsp plain flour

salt and pepper

1.25 kg/2 lb 12 oz stewing steak, cut into cubes

425 ml/15 fl oz stout

2 tsp muscovado sugar

2 bay leaves

1 tbsp chopped fresh thyme

for the herb dumplings

115 g/4 oz self-raising flour

pinch of salt

55 g/2 oz shredded suet

2 tbsp chopped fresh parsley, plus extra to garnish

about 4 tbsp water

Daube of Beef

Combine the wine, brandy, vinegar, shallots, carrots, garlic, peppercorns, thyme, rosemary, parsley and bay leaf, and season to taste with salt. Add the beef, stirring to coat, then cover with clingfilm and leave in the refrigerator to marinate for 8 hours, or overnight.

Preheat the oven to 150°C/300°F/Gas Mark 2. Drain the beef, reserving the marinade, and pat dry on kitchen paper. Heat half the oil in a large, flameproof casserole. Add the beef in batches and cook over a medium heat, stirring, for 3–4 minutes, or until browned. Transfer the beef to a plate with a slotted spoon. Brown the remaining beef, adding more oil, if necessary.

Return all of the beef to the casserole and add the tomatoes and their juices, mushrooms and orange rind. Sieve the reserved marinade into the casserole. Bring to the boil, cover and cook in the preheated oven for 2½ hours.

Remove the casserole from the oven, add the ham and olives and return it to the oven to cook for a further 30 minutes, or until the beef is very tender. Discard the orange rind and serve straight from the casserole, garnished with parsley.

SERVES 6

350 ml/12 fl oz dry white wine

2 tbsp brandy

1 tbsp white wine vinegar

4 shallots, sliced

4 carrots, sliced

1 garlic clove, finely chopped

6 black peppercorns

4 fresh thyme sprigs

1 fresh rosemary sprig

2 fresh parsley sprigs, plus extra
    to garnish

1 bay leaf

salt

750 g/1 lb 10 oz beef topside, cut
    into 2.5-cm/1-inch cubes

2 tbsp olive oil

800 g/1 lb 12 oz canned chopped
    tomatoes

225 g/8 oz mushrooms, sliced

strips of finely pared orange rind

55 g/2 oz Bayonne ham, cut
    into strips

12 black olives

Beef Goulash

Heat the vegetable oil in a large frying pan and cook the onion and garlic for 3–4 minutes.

Cut the stewing steak into chunks and cook over a high heat for 3 minutes until browned all over. Add the paprika and stir well, then add the chopped tomatoes, tomato purée, pepper and mushrooms. Cook for 2 minutes, stirring frequently.

Pour in the beef stock. Bring to the boil, then reduce the heat. Cover and simmer for 1½–2 hours until the meat is tender.

Blend the cornflour with the water, then add to the pan, stirring until thickened and smooth. Cook for 1 minute, then season with salt and pepper to taste.

Put the natural yogurt in a serving bowl and sprinkle with a little paprika.

Transfer the beef goulash to a warmed serving dish, garnish with chopped fresh parsley and serve with rice and yogurt.

SERVES 4

2 tbsp vegetable oil

1 large onion, chopped

1 garlic clove, crushed

750 g/1 lb 10 oz lean stewing steak

2 tbsp paprika

425 g/15 oz canned chopped tomatoes

2 tbsp tomato purée

1 large red pepper, deseeded and chopped

175 g/6 oz mushrooms, sliced

600 ml/1 pint beef stock

1 tbsp cornflour

1 tbsp water

salt and pepper

4 tbsp natural yogurt

paprika, for sprinkling

chopped fresh parsley, to garnish

freshly cooked long-grain and wild rice, to serve

Irish Stew

Preheat the oven to 160°C/325°F/Gas Mark 3. Spread the flour on a plate and season with salt and pepper. Roll the pieces of lamb in the flour to coat, shaking off any excess, and arrange in the base of a casserole.

Layer the onions, carrots and potatoes on top of the lamb.

Sprinkle in the thyme and pour in the stock, then cover and cook in the preheated oven for 2$^1/_2$ hours. Garnish with the chopped fresh parsley and serve straight from the casserole.

SERVES 4

4 tbsp plain flour

salt and pepper

1.3 kg/3 lb middle neck of lamb, trimmed of visible fat and cut into pieces

3 large onions, chopped

3 carrots, sliced

450 g/1 lb potatoes, quartered

$^1/_2$ tsp dried thyme

850 ml/1$^1/_2$ pints hot lamb stock

2 tbsp chopped fresh parsley, to garnish

Lamb Stew with Chickpeas

Preheat the oven to 160°C/325°F/Gas Mark 3. Heat 4 tablespoons of the oil in a large, heavy-based flameproof casserole over a medium–high heat. Reduce the heat, add the chorizo and fry for 1 minute and then set aside. Add the onions to the casserole and fry for 2 minutes, then add the garlic and continue frying for 3 minutes, or until the onions are soft, but not brown. Remove from the casserole and set aside.

Heat the remaining 2 tablespoons of oil in the casserole. Add the lamb cubes in a single layer without over-crowding the casserole, and fry until browned on each side; work in batches, if necessary.

Return the onion mixture to the casserole with all the lamb. Stir in the stock, wine, vinegar, tomatoes with their juices and salt and pepper to taste. Bring to the boil, scraping any glazed bits from the base of the casserole. Reduce the heat and stir in the thyme, bay leaves and paprika.

Transfer to the preheated oven and cook, covered, for 40–45 minutes until the lamb is tender. Stir in the chickpeas and return to the oven, uncovered, for 10 minutes, or until they are heated through and the juices are reduced.

Taste and adjust the seasoning. Serve garnished with thyme.

SERVES 4–6

6 tbsp olive oil

225 g/8 oz chorizo sausage, cut into 5-mm/^{1}/$_4$-inch thick slices, casings removed

2 large onions, chopped

6 large garlic cloves, crushed

900 g/2 lb boned leg of lamb, cut into 5-cm/2-inch cubes

250 ml/9 fl oz lamb stock or water

125 ml/4 fl oz red wine, such as Rioja or Tempranillo

2 tbsp sherry vinegar

000 g/1 lb 12 oz canned chopped tomatoes

salt and pepper

4 sprigs fresh thyme, plus extra to garnish

2 bay leaves

^{1}/$_2$ tsp sweet Spanish paprika

800 g/1 lb 12 oz canned chickpeas, rinsed and drained

Lamb with Pears

Preheat the oven to 160°C/325°F/Gas Mark 3. Heat the olive oil in a flameproof casserole over a medium heat. Add the lamb and cook, turning frequently, for 5–10 minutes, or until browned on all sides.

Arrange the pear quarters on top, then sprinkle over the ginger. Cover with the potatoes. Pour in the cider and season to taste with salt and pepper. Cover and cook in the preheated oven for 1^1/$_4$ hours.

Trim the stalk ends of the green beans. Remove the casserole from the oven and add the beans, then re-cover and return to the oven for a further 30 minutes. Taste and adjust the seasoning. Sprinkle with the chives and serve.

SERVES 4

1 tbsp olive oil

1 kg/2 lb 4 oz best end-of-neck lamb
   cutlets, trimmed of visible fat

6 pears, peeled, cored and
   quartered

1 tsp ground ginger

4 potatoes, diced

4 tbsp dry cider

salt and pepper

450 g/1 lb green beans

2 tbsp snipped fresh chives,
   to garnish

Pork & Vegetable Ragout

Trim off and discard any fat or gristle from the pork and cut the meat into thin strips about 5 cm/2 inch long. Mix the flour and spices together. Toss the pork in the spiced flour until well coated and reserve any remaining spiced flour.

Heat the oil in a large, heavy-based saucepan and cook the onion, stirring frequently, for 5 minutes, or until softened. Add the pork and cook over a high heat, stirring frequently, for 5 minutes, or until browned on all sides and sealed. Sprinkle in the reserved spiced flour and cook, stirring constantly, for 2 minutes, then remove from the heat.

Gradually stir in the tomatoes. Blend the tomato purée with a little of the stock in a jug and gradually stir into the saucepan, then stir in half the remaining stock

Add the carrots, then return to the heat and bring to the boil, stirring. Reduce the heat, cover and simmer, stirring occasionally, for 1¹/2 hours. Add the squash and cook for a further 15 minutes.

Add the leeks and okra, and the remaining stock if you prefer a thinner ragout. Simmer for a further 15 minutes, or until the pork and vegetables are tender. Season to taste with salt and pepper, then garnish with fresh parsley and serve with couscous.

SERVES 4

450 g/1 lb lean boneless pork

1¹/2 tbsp plain flour

1 tsp ground coriander

1 tsp ground cumin

1¹/2 tsp ground cinnamon

1 tbsp olive oil

1 onion, chopped

400 g/14 oz canned chopped
   tomatoes

2 tbsp tomato purée

300–450 ml/10–16 fl oz chicken
   stock

225 g/8 oz carrots, chopped

350 g/12 oz squash, such as
   kabocha, peeled, deseeded and
   chopped

225 g/8 oz leeks, sliced, blanched
   and drained

115 g/4 oz okra, trimmed and sliced

salt and pepper

fresh parsley sprigs, to garnish

couscous, to serve

Sausage & Bean Casserole

Prick the sausages all over with a fork. Heat 2 tablespoons of the oil in a large, heavy-based frying pan. Add the sausages and cook over low heat, turning frequently, for 10–15 minutes, until evenly browned and cooked through. Remove them from the frying pan and keep warm. Drain off the oil and wipe out the pan with kitchen paper.

Heat the remaining oil in the frying pan. Add the onion, garlic and pepper to the frying pan and cook for 5 minutes, stirring occasionally, or until softened.

Add the tomatoes to the frying pan and leave the mixture to simmer for about 5 minutes, stirring occasionally, or until slightly reduced and thickened.

Stir the sun-dried tomato paste, cannellini beans and sausages into the mixture in the frying pan. Cook for 4–5 minutes or until the mixture is piping hot. Add 4–5 tablespoons of water, if the mixture becomes too dry during cooking.

Transfer the sausage and bean casserole to serving plates and serve with mashed potatoes or rice.

SERVES 4

8 sausages

3 tbsp olive oil

1 large onion, chopped

2 garlic cloves, chopped

1 green pepper, deseeded and sliced

225 g/8 oz fresh tomatoes, skinned and chopped or 400 g/14 oz canned tomatoes, chopped

2 tbsp sun-dried tomato paste

400 g/14 oz canned cannellini beans

mashed potatoes or freshly cooked rice, to serve

Red Curry Pork with Peppers

Heat the oil in a wok or large frying pan and fry the onion and garlic for 1–2 minutes, until they are softened but not browned.

Add the pork slices and stir-fry for 2–3 minutes until browned all over. Add the pepper, mushrooms and curry paste.

Dissolve the coconut in the stock and add to the wok with the soy sauce. Bring to the boil and simmer for 4–5 minutes or until the liquid has reduced and thickened.

Add the tomatoes and coriander and cook for 1–2 minutes before serving with noodles or rice.

SERVES 4

2 tbsp vegetable or groundnut oil

1 onion, roughly chopped

2 garlic cloves, chopped

450 g/1 lb pork fillet, sliced thickly·

1 red pepper, deseeded and cut into squares

175 g/6 oz mushrooms, quartered

2 tbsp Thai red curry paste

115 g/4 oz creamed coconut, chopped

300 ml/$\frac{1}{2}$ pint pork or vegetable stock

2 tbsp Thai soy sauce

4 tomatoes, peeled, deseeded and chopped

handful of fresh coriander, chopped

boiled noodles or rice, to serve

Poultry Pot Wonders

One-pot cooking is the perfect technique for poultry, especially chicken, which can sometimes be disappointingly bland and dry when cooked in other ways. Fabulous stews and aromatic curries burst with flavour and vitality. Discover the versatility of poultry with these inspiring international recipes for chicken, turkey and duck.

Coq au Vin

Melt half the butter with the olive oil in a large, flameproof casserole. Add the chicken and cook over a medium heat, stirring, for 8–10 minutes, or until golden brown all over. Add the bacon, onions, mushrooms and garlic.

Pour in the brandy and set it alight with a match or taper. When the flames have died down, add the wine, stock and bouquet garni and season to taste with salt and pepper. Bring to the boil, reduce the heat and simmer gently for 1 hour, or until the chicken pieces are cooked through and tender. Meanwhile, make a beurre manié by mashing the remaining butter with the flour in a small bowl.

Remove and discard the bouquet garni. Transfer the chicken to a large plate and keep warm. Stir the beurre manié into the casserole, a little at a time. Bring to the boil, return the chicken to the casserole and serve immediately, garnished with bay leaves.

SERVES 4

55 g/2 oz butter

2 tbsp olive oil

1.8 kg/4 lb chicken pieces

115 g/4 oz rindless smoked bacon,
    cut into strips

115 g/4 oz baby onions

115 g/4 oz chestnut mushrooms,
    halved

2 garlic cloves, finely chopped

2 tbsp brandy

225 ml/8 fl oz red wine

300 ml/10 fl oz chicken stock

1 bouquet garni

salt and pepper

2 tbsp plain flour

bay leaves, to garnish

Brunswick Stew

Season the chicken pieces with salt and dust with paprika.

Heat the oil and butter in a flameproof casserole or large saucepan. Add the chicken pieces and cook over a medium heat, turning, for 10–15 minutes, or until golden. Transfer to a plate with a slotted spoon.

Add the onion and peppers to the casserole. Cook over a low heat, stirring occasionally, for 5 minutes, or until softened. Add the tomatoes, wine, stock, Worcestershire sauce, Tabasco sauce and parsley and bring to the boil, stirring. Return the chicken to the casserole, cover and simmer, stirring occasionally, for 30 minutes.

Add the sweetcorn and beans to the casserole, partially re-cover and simmer for a further 30 minutes. Place the flour and water in a small bowl and mix to make a paste. Stir a ladleful of the cooking liquid into the paste, then stir it into the stew. Cook, stirring frequently, for 5 minutes. Serve, garnished with parsley.

SERVES 6

1.8 kg/4 lb chicken pieces

salt

2 tbsp paprika

2 tbsp olive oil

25 g/1 oz butter

450 g/1 lb onions, chopped

2 yellow peppers, deseeded and chopped

400 g/14 oz canned chopped tomatoes

225 ml/8 fl oz dry white wine

450 ml/16 fl oz chicken stock

1 tbsp Worcestershire sauce

$^{1}/_{2}$ tsp Tabasco sauce

1 tbsp finely chopped fresh parsley

325 g/11$^{1}/_{2}$ oz canned sweetcorn kernels, drained

425 g/15 oz canned butter beans, drained and rinsed

2 tbsp plain flour

4 tbsp water

freshly chopped parsley, to garnish

Chicken Tagine

Heat the oil in a large saucepan over a medium heat, add the onion and garlic and cook for 3 minutes, stirring frequently. Add the chicken and cook, stirring constantly, for a further 5 minutes, or until sealed on all sides. Add the cumin and cinnamon sticks to the saucepan halfway through sealing the chicken.

Sprinkle in the flour and cook, stirring constantly, for 2 minutes.

Add the aubergine, red pepper and mushrooms and cook for a further 2 minutes, stirring constantly.

Blend the tomato purée with the stock, stir into the saucepan and bring to the boil. Reduce the heat and add the chickpeas and apricots. Cover and simmer for 15–20 minutes, or until the chicken is tender.

Season with salt and pepper to taste and serve immediately, sprinkled with coriander.

SERVES 4

1 tbsp olive oil

1 onion, cut into small wedges

2–4 garlic cloves, sliced

450 g/1 lb skinless, boneless chicken breast, diced

1 tsp ground cumin

2 cinnamon sticks, lightly bruised

1 tbsp plain wholemeal flour

225 g/8 oz aubergine, diced

1 red pepper, deseeded and chopped

85 g/3 oz button mushrooms, sliced

1 tbsp tomato purée

600 ml/1 pint chicken stock

280 g/10 oz canned chickpeas, drained and rinsed

55 g/2 oz no-soak dried apricots, chopped

salt and pepper

1 tbsp chopped fresh coriander, to garnish

Balti Chicken

Heat the ghee in a large, heavy-based frying pan. Add the onions and cook over a low heat, stirring occasionally, for 10 minutes, or until golden. Add the sliced tomatoes, kalonji seeds, peppercorns, cardamoms, cinnamon stick, chilli powder, garam masala, garlic paste and ginger paste, and season with salt to taste. Cook, stirring constantly, for 5 minutes.

Add the chicken and cook, stirring constantly, for 5 minutes, or until well coated in the spice paste. Stir in the yogurt. Cover and simmer, stirring occasionally, for 10 minutes.

Stir in the chopped coriander, chillies and lime juice. Transfer to a warmed serving dish, sprinkle with more chopped coriander and serve immediately.

SERVES 6

3 tbsp ghee or vegetable oil

2 large onions, sliced

3 tomatoes, sliced

$1/2$ tsp kalonji seeds

4 black peppercorns

2 cardamom pods

1 cinnamon stick

1 tsp chilli powder

1 tsp garam masala

1 tsp garlic paste

1 tsp ginger paste

salt

700 g/1 lb 9 oz skinless, boneless chicken breasts or thighs, diced

2 tbsp natural yogurt

2 tbsp chopped fresh coriander, plus extra to garnish

2 fresh green chillies, deseeded and finely chopped

2 tbsp lime juice

Louisiana Chicken

Heat the oil in a large, heavy-based saucepan or flameproof casserole. Add the chicken and cook over a medium heat, stirring, for 5–10 minutes, or until golden. Transfer the chicken to a plate with a slotted spoon.

Stir the flour into the oil and cook over a very low heat, stirring constantly, for 15 minutes, or until light golden. Do not let it burn. Immediately, add the onion, celery and green pepper and cook, stirring constantly, for 2 minutes. Add the garlic, thyme and chillies and cook, stirring, for 1 minute.

Stir in the tomatoes and their juices, then gradually stir in the stock. Return the chicken pieces to the saucepan, cover and simmer for 45 minutes, or until the chicken is cooked through and tender. Season to taste with salt and pepper, transfer to warmed serving plates and serve immediately, garnished with some lettuce leaves and a sprinkling of chopped thyme.

SERVES 4

5 tbsp sunflower oil

4 chicken portions

55 g/2 oz plain flour

1 onion, chopped

2 celery sticks, sliced

1 green pepper, deseeded and chopped

2 garlic cloves, finely chopped

2 tsp chopped fresh thyme

2 fresh red chillies, deseeded and finely chopped

400 g/14 oz canned chopped tomatoes

300 ml/10 fl oz chicken stock

salt and pepper

lamb's lettuce, to garnish

chopped fresh thyme, to garnish

Chicken with Garlic

Sift the flour on to a large plate and season with paprika and salt and pepper to taste. Dredge the chicken pieces with the flour on both sides, shaking off the excess.

Heat 4 tablespoons of the oil in a large, deep frying pan or flameproof casserole over a medium heat. Add the garlic and fry, stirring frequently, for about 2 minutes to flavour the oil. Remove with a slotted spoon and set aside to drain on kitchen paper.

Add as many chicken pieces, skin-side down, as will fit in a single layer. Work in batches if necessary, to avoid over-crowding the frying pan, adding a little extra oil if necessary. Fry for 5 minutes until the skin is golden brown. Turn over and fry for 5 minutes longer.

Pour off any excess oil. Return the garlic and chicken pieces to the frying pan and add the chicken stock, wine and herbs. Bring to the boil, then reduce the heat, cover and simmer for 20–25 minutes until the chicken is cooked through and tender and the garlic is very soft.

Transfer the chicken pieces to a serving platter and keep warm. Bring the cooking liquid to the boil, with the garlic and herbs, and boil until reduced to about 300 ml/½ pint. Remove and discard the cooked herbs. Taste and adjust the seasoning, if necessary.

Spoon the sauce and the garlic cloves over the chicken pieces. Garnish with fresh parsley and thyme, and serve.

SERVES 4

4 tbsp plain flour

Spanish paprika, either hot or
  smoked sweet, to taste

salt and pepper

1 large chicken, about 1.75 kg/
  3 lb 12 oz, cut into 8 pieces,
  rinsed and patted dry

4–6 tbsp olive oil

24 large garlic cloves, peeled and
  halved

450 ml/$^3/_4$ pint chicken stock,
  preferably home-made

4 tbsp dry white wine, such as white
  Rioja

2 sprigs of fresh flat-leaf parsley,
  1 bay leaf and 1 sprig of fresh
  thyme, tied together

fresh flat-leaf parsley and thyme
  leaves, to garnish

Italian Turkey Steaks

Preheat the grill to medium. Heat the oil in a flameproof casserole or heavy-based frying pan. Add the turkey escalopes and cook over a medium heat for 5–10 minutes, turning occasionally, until golden. Transfer to a plate.

Add the red peppers and onion to the frying pan and cook over a low heat, stirring occasionally, for 5 minutes, or until softened. Add the garlic and cook for a further 2 minutes.

Return the turkey to the frying pan and add the passata, wine and marjoram. Season to taste with salt and pepper. Bring to the boil, then reduce the heat, cover and simmer, stirring occasionally, for 25–30 minutes, or until the turkey is cooked through and tender.

Stir in the cannellini beans and simmer for a further 5 minutes. Sprinkle the breadcrumbs over the top and place under the preheated grill for 2–3 minutes, or until golden. Serve, garnished with fresh basil sprigs.

SERVES 4

1 tbsp olive oil

4 turkey escalopes or steaks

2 red peppers, deseeded and sliced

1 red onion, sliced

2 garlic cloves, finely chopped

300 ml/10 fl oz passata

150 ml/5 fl oz medium white wine

1 tbsp chopped fresh marjoram

salt and pepper

400 g/14 oz canned cannellini
   beans, drained and rinsed

3 tbsp fresh white breadcrumbs

fresh basil sprigs, to garnish

Duck Legs with Olives

Put the duck legs in the bottom of a flameproof casserole or a large, heavy-based frying pan with a tight-fitting lid, over a medium–low heat. Add the tomatoes, garlic, onion, carrot, celery, thyme and olives and stir together. Season with salt and pepper to taste.

Turn the heat to high and cook, uncovered, until the ingredients begin to bubble. Reduce the heat to low, cover tightly and simmer for 1¼–1½ hours until the duck is very tender. Check occasionally and add a little water if the mixture appears to be drying out.

When the duck legs are tender, transfer them to a serving platter, cover and keep hot in a warmed oven. Leave the rest of the casserole uncovered, increase the heat to medium and cook, stirring, for about 10 minutes until the mixture forms a sauce. Stir in the orange rind, then taste and adjust the seasoning if necessary.

Mash the tender garlic cloves with a fork and spread over the duck legs. Spoon the sauce over the top and serve at once.

SERVES 4

4 duck legs, all visible fat removed
   and discarded
800 g/1 lb 12 oz canned tomatoes,
   chopped
8 garlic cloves, peeled, but left whole
1 large onion, chopped
1 carrot, peeled and chopped finely
1 celery stick, peeled and chopped
   finely
3 sprigs fresh thyme
100 g/3½ oz Spanish green olives in
   brine, stuffed with pimientos, garlic
   or almonds, drained and rinsed
salt and pepper
1 tsp finely grated orange rind

Fish & Seafood Suppers

From fiery fish curries to hearty stews, these dishes prove once and for all that cooking and eating fish is not a chore, but a pleasure. For many of us, fish and seafood, with its light fresh taste, may be something we only eat on our summer holidays. However, these recipes demonstrate how well it takes on more robust flavours, making it perfect for winter dishes too. Classic fish and seafood dishes are the perfect choice for impressive entertaining and the quicker cooking time also makes for speedy suppers.

Hearty Fish Stew

Put the saffron threads in a heatproof jug with the water and leave for at least 10 minutes to infuse.

Heat the oil in a large, heavy-based flameproof casserole over a medium–high heat. Reduce the heat to low and cook the onion, stirring occasionally, for 10 minutes, or until golden but not browned. Stir in the garlic, thyme, bay leaves and red peppers and cook, stirring frequently, for 5 minutes, or until the peppers are softened and the onions have softened further.

Add the tomatoes and paprika and simmer, stirring frequently, for a further 5 minutes.

Stir in the stock, the saffron and its soaking liquid and the almonds and bring to the boil, stirring. Reduce the heat and simmer for 5–10 minutes, until the sauce reduces and thickens. Season to taste with salt and pepper.

Meanwhile, clean the mussels and clams by scrubbing or scraping the shells and pull out any beards that are attached to the mussels. Discard any with broken shells or any that refuse to close when tapped.

Gently stir the hake into the stew so that it doesn't break up, then add the prawns, mussels and clams. Reduce the heat to very low, cover and simmer for 5 minutes, or until the hake is opaque, the mussels and clams have opened and the prawns have turned pink. Discard any mussels or clams that remain closed. Serve immediately with plenty of thick crusty bread for soaking up the juices.

SERVES 4–6

large pinch of saffron threads

4 tbsp almost-boiling water

6 tbsp olive oil

1 large onion, chopped

2 garlic cloves, finely chopped

1½ tbsp chopped fresh thyme leaves

2 bay leaves

2 red peppers, deseeded and roughly chopped

800 g/1 lb 12 oz canned chopped tomatoes

1 tsp smoked paprika

250 ml/9 fl oz fish stock

140 g/5 oz blanched almonds, toasted and finely ground

salt and pepper

12–16 live mussels

12–16 live clams

600 g/1 lb 5 oz thick boned hake or cod fillets, skinned and cut into 5-cm/2-inch chunks

12–16 raw prawns, peeled and deveined

thick crusty bread, to serve

Seafood Hotpot with Red Wine & Tomatoes

Remove the beards from the mussels. Rinse the mussels well, to remove any sand, and discard any with broken shells or that remain open when tapped.

Heat the oil in a heavy-based saucepan or flameproof casserole over a medium heat and add the onion and pepper. Cook for 5 minutes, or until beginning to soften.

Stir in the garlic, tomato purée, parsley and oregano. Cook for 1 minute, stirring.

Pour in the tomatoes and wine. Season with salt and pepper. Bring to the boil, then cover and simmer over a low heat for 30 minutes. Add the fish, then cover and simmer for 15 minutes.

Add the mussels, scallops, prawns and crab meat. Cover and cook for 15 minutes more. Discard any mussels that have not opened.

Stir in the basil and serve immediately.

SERVES 4–6

350 g/12 oz live mussels, scrubbed

4 tbsp olive oil

1 onion, chopped finely

1 green pepper, deseeded and chopped

2 garlic cloves, chopped very finely

5 tbsp tomato purée

1 tbsp chopped fresh flat-leaf parsley

1 tsp dried oregano

400 g/14 oz canned chopped tomatoes

225 ml/8 fl oz dry red wine

salt and pepper

450 g/1 lb firm white fish, such as cod or monkfish, cut into 5 cm/ 2 inch pieces

115 g/4 oz scallops, halved

115 g/4 oz raw prawns, peeled

200 g/7 oz canned crab meat

10–15 fresh basil leaves, shredded, to garnish

Seafood in Saffron Sauce

Clean the mussels and clams by scrubbing or scraping the shells and pull out any beards that are attached to the mussels. Discard any with broken shells or any that refuse to close when tapped.

Heat the oil in a large, flameproof casserole and cook the onion with the saffron, thyme and a pinch of salt over a low heat, stirring occasionally, for 5 minutes, or until softened. Add the garlic and cook, stirring, for 2 minutes.

Add the tomatoes, wine and stock, season to taste with salt and pepper and stir well. Bring to the boil, then reduce the heat and simmer for 15 minutes.

Add the fish chunks and simmer for a further 3 minutes. Add the mussels, clams and squid rings and simmer for a further 5 minutes, or until the mussels and clams have opened. Discard any that remain closed. Stir in the basil and serve immediately, accompanied by plenty of fresh bread to mop up the broth.

SERVES 4

225 g/8 oz live mussels

225 g/8 oz live clams

2 tbsp olive oil

1 onion, sliced

pinch of saffron threads

1 tbsp chopped fresh thyme

salt and pepper

2 garlic cloves, finely chopped

800 g/1 lb 12 oz canned tomatoes, drained and chopped

175 ml/6 fl oz dry white wine

2 litres/$3^1/2$ pints fish stock

350 g/12 oz red mullet fillets, cut into bite-sized chunks

450 g/1 lb monkfish fillets, cut into bite-sized chunks

225 g/8 oz raw squid rings

2 tbsp fresh shredded basil leaves

fresh bread, to serve

Seafood Chilli

Place the prawns, scallops, monkfish chunks and lime slices in a large, non-metallic dish with ¼ teaspoon of the chilli powder, ¼ teaspoon of the ground cumin, 1 tablespoon of the chopped coriander, half the garlic, the fresh chilli and 1 tablespoon of the oil. Cover with clingfilm and leave to marinate for up to 1 hour.

Meanwhile, heat 1 tablespoon of the remaining oil in a flameproof casserole or large, heavy-based saucepan. Add the onion, the remaining garlic and the red and yellow peppers and cook over a low heat, stirring occasionally, for 5 minutes, or until softened. Add the remaining chilli powder, the remaining cumin, the cloves, cinnamon and cayenne pepper with the remaining oil, if necessary, and season to taste with salt. Cook, stirring, for 5 minutes, then gradually stir in the stock and the tomatoes and their juices. Partially cover and simmer for 25 minutes.

Add the beans to the tomato mixture and spoon the fish and shellfish on top. Cover and cook for 10 minutes, or until the fish and shellfish are cooked through. Sprinkle with the remaining coriander and serve.

SERVES 4

115 g/4 oz raw prawns, peeled

250 g/9 oz prepared scallops, thawed if frozen

115 g/4 oz monkfish fillet, cut into chunks

1 lime, peeled and thinly sliced

1 tbsp chilli powder

1 tsp ground cumin

3 tbsp chopped fresh coriander

2 garlic cloves, finely chopped

1 fresh green chilli, deseeded and chopped

3 tbsp corn oil

1 onion, roughly chopped

1 red pepper, deseeded and roughly chopped

1 yellow pepper, deseeded and roughly chopped

¼ tsp ground cloves

pinch of ground cinnamon

pinch of cayenne pepper

salt

350 ml/12 fl oz fish stock

400 g/14 oz canned chopped tomatoes

400 g/14 oz canned red kidney beans, drained and rinsed

Seafood Curry

Heat the oil in a kadhai, wok or large frying pan over a high heat. Add the mustard seeds and stir them around for about 1 minute, or until they jump. Stir in the curry leaves.

Add the shallots and garlic and stir for about 5 minutes, or until the shallots are golden. Stir in the turmeric, coriander and chilli powder and continue stirring for about 30 seconds.

Add the dissolved creamed coconut. Bring to the boil, then reduce the heat to medium and stir for about 2 minutes.

Reduce the heat to low, add the fish and simmer for 1 minute, spooning the sauce over the fish and very gently stirring it around. Add the prawns and continue to simmer for 4–5 minutes longer until the fish flesh flakes easily and the prawns turn pink and curl.

Add half the lime juice, then taste and add more lime juice and salt to taste, if necessary. Sprinkle the lime rind over the top and serve with lime wedges.

SERVES 4–6

3 tbsp vegetable or groundnut oil

1 tbsp black mustard seeds

12 fresh curry leaves or 1 tbsp dried

6 shallots, finely chopped

1 garlic clove, crushed

1 tsp ground turmeric

$^1/_2$ ground coriander

$^1/_4$–$^1/_2$ tsp chilli powder

140 g/5 oz creamed coconut, grated and dissolved in 300 ml/10 fl oz boiling water

500 g/1 lb 2 oz skinless, boneless white fish, such as monkfish or cod, cut into large chunks

450 g/1 lb large raw prawns, peeled and deveined

finely grated rind and juice of 1 lime

salt

lime wedges, to serve

Spicy Monkfish Rice

Process the chilli, chilli flakes, garlic, saffron, mint, olive oil and lemon juice in a food processor or blender until combined, but not smooth.

Put the monkfish into a non-metallic dish and pour over the spice paste, turning to coat. Cover and set aside for 20 minutes to marinate.

Heat a large pan until very hot. Using a slotted spoon, lift the monkfish from the marinade and add, in batches, to the hot pan. Cook for 3–4 minutes until browned and firm. Remove with a draining spoon and set aside.

Add the onion and remaining marinade to the pan and cook for 5 minutes until softened and lightly browned. Add the rice and stir until well coated. Add the tomatoes and coconut milk. Bring to the boil, cover and simmer very gently for 15 minutes. Stir in the peas, season and arrange the fish over the top. Cover with foil and continue to cook over a very low heat for 5 minutes. Serve garnished with the chopped mint.

SERVES 4

1 fresh hot red chilli, deseeded
   and chopped
1 tsp chilli flakes
2 garlic cloves, chopped
pinch of saffron
3 tbsp roughly chopped fresh
   mint leaves
4 tbsp olive oil
2 tbsp lemon juice
375 g/12 oz monkfish fillet,
   cut into bite-sized pieces
1 onion, chopped finely
225 g/8 oz long-grain rice
400g/14 oz canned chopped
   tomatoes
200 ml/7 fl oz coconut milk
115 g/4 oz peas
salt and pepper
2 tbsp chopped fresh mint,
   to garnish

Prawn Biryani

Soak the saffron in the tepid water for 20 minutes. Put the shallots, garlic, spices and salt into a spice grinder or mortar and pestle and grind to a paste.

Heat the ghee in a saucepan and add the mustard seeds. When they start to pop, add the prawns and stir over a high heat for 1 minute. Stir in the spice mix, then the coconut milk and yogurt. Simmer for 20 minutes.

Spoon the prawn mixture into serving bowls. Top with the freshly cooked basmati rice and drizzle over the saffron water. Serve, garnished with the flaked almonds, spring onion and sprigs of coriander.

SERVES 8

1 tsp saffron strands

50 ml/2 fl oz tepid water

2 shallots, chopped coarsely

3 garlic cloves, crushed

1 tsp chopped fresh root ginger

2 tsp coriander seeds

$^1/_2$ tsp black peppercorns

2 cloves

seeds from 2 green cardamom pods

2.5-cm/1-inch piece cinnamon stick

1 tsp ground turmeric

1 fresh green chilli, chopped

$^1/_2$ tsp salt

2 tbsp ghee

1 tsp whole black mustard seeds

500 g/1 lb 2 oz uncooked tiger
    prawns in their shells, or
    400 g/14 oz uncooked and peeled

300 ml/$^1/_2$ pint coconut milk

300 ml/$^1/_2$ pint low-fat natural
    yogurt

freshly cooked basmati rice,
    to serve

to garnish

flaked almonds, toasted

1 spring onion, sliced

sprigs of fresh coriander

Vegetable Heaven

Eating plenty of healthy vegetables every day could not be easier or more fun than with this superb collection of international recipes. Whether your taste is for a hearty bean stew, an aromatic curry or a satisfying risotto, these delicious and easy-to-prepare vegetable dishes are sure to fit the bill. Economical, irresistible, nourishing and all in a single pot – what more could anyone want?

Tuscan Bean Stew

Trim the fennel and reserve any feathery fronds, then cut the bulb into small strips. Heat the oil in a large, heavy-based saucepan with a tight-fitting lid, and cook the onion, garlic, chilli and fennel strips, stirring frequently, for 5–8 minutes, or until softened.

Add the aubergine and cook, stirring frequently, for 5 minutes. Blend the tomato purée with a little of the stock in a jug and pour over the fennel mixture, then add the remaining stock, and the tomatoes, vinegar and oregano. Bring to the boil, then reduce the heat, cover and simmer for 15 minutes, or until the tomatoes have begun to collapse.

Drain and rinse the beans, then drain again. Add them to the pan with the yellow pepper, courgette and olives. Simmer for a further 15 minutes, or until all the vegetables are tender. Taste and adjust the seasoning. Scatter with the Parmesan cheese shavings and serve garnished with the reserved fennel fronds, accompanied by crusty bread.

SERVES 4

1 large fennel bulb

2 tbsp olive oil

1 red onion, cut into small wedges

2–4 garlic cloves, sliced

1 fresh green chilli, deseeded and
  chopped

1 small aubergine, about 225 g/
  8 oz, cut into chunks

2 tbsp tomato purée

450–600 ml/16 fl oz–1 pint
  vegetable stock

450 g/1 lb ripe tomatoes

1 tbsp balsamic vinegar

a few sprigs fresh oregano

400 g/14 oz canned borlotti beans

400 g/14 oz canned flageolet beans

1 yellow pepper, deseeded and cut
  into small strips

1 courgette, sliced into half moons

55 g/2 oz stoned black olives

salt and pepper

25 g/1 oz Parmesan cheese, freshly
  shaved

crusty bread or polenta wedges,
  to serve

Vegetable Goulash

Put the sun-dried tomatoes in a small heatproof bowl, cover with almost boiling water and leave to soak for 15–20 minutes. Drain, reserving the soaking liquid.

Heat the oil in a large, heavy-based saucepan, with a tight-fitting lid, and cook the chillies, garlic and vegetables, stirring frequently, for 5–8 minutes until softened. Blend the tomato purée with a little of the stock in a jug and pour over the vegetable mixture, then add the remaining stock, lentils, the sun-dried tomatoes and their soaking liquid, and the paprika and thyme.

Bring to the boil, then reduce the heat, cover and simmer for 15 minutes. Add the fresh tomatoes and simmer for a further 15 minutes, or until the vegetables and lentils are tender. Serve topped with spoonfuls of soured cream, accompanied by crusty bread.

SERVES 4

15 g/^{1}/$_2$ oz sun-dried tomatoes, chopped

2 tbsp olive oil

^{1}/$_2$–1 tsp crushed dried chillies

2–3 garlic cloves, chopped

1 large onion, cut into small wedges

1 small celeriac, cut into small chunks

225 g/8 oz carrots, sliced

225 g/8 oz new potatoes, scrubbed and cut into chunks

1 small acorn squash, deseeded, peeled and cut into small chunks, about 225 g/8 oz prepared weight

2 tbsp tomato purée

300 ml/10 fl oz vegetable stock

450 g/1 lb canned Puy or green lentils, drained and rinsed

1–2 tsp hot paprika

a few sprigs fresh thyme

450 g/1 lb ripe tomatoes

soured cream, to garnish

crusty bread, to serve

Spicy Vegetable Stew

Heat the oil in a large, heavy-based saucepan with a tight-fitting lid and cook the onion, garlic, chilli and aubergine, stirring frequently, for 5–8 minutes until softened.

Add the ginger, cumin, coriander and saffron and cook, stirring constantly, for 2 minutes. Bruise the cinnamon.

Add the cinnamon, squash, sweet potatoes, prunes, stock and tomatoes to the saucepan and bring to the boil. Reduce the heat, cover and simmer, stirring occasionally, for 20 minutes. Add the chickpeas to the saucepan and cook for a further 10 minutes. Discard the cinnamon and serve garnished with the fresh coriander.

SERVES 4

2 tbsp olive oil

1 Spanish onion, finely chopped

2–4 garlic cloves, crushed

1 fresh red chilli, deseeded and sliced

1 aubergine, about 225 g/8 oz, cut into small chunks

small piece fresh root ginger, peeled and grated

1 tsp ground cumin

1 tsp ground coriander

pinch of saffron threads or $1/2$ tsp turmeric

1–2 cinnamon sticks

$1/2$–1 butternut squash, about 450 g/1 lb, peeled, deseeded and cut into small chunks

225 g/8 oz sweet potatoes, cut into small chunks

85 g/3 oz ready-to-eat prunes

450–600 ml/16 fl oz–1 pint vegetable stock

4 tomatoes, chopped

400 g/14 oz canned chickpeas, drained and rinsed

1 tbsp chopped fresh coriander, to garnish

Chilli Bean Stew

Heat the oil in a large, heavy-based saucepan with a tight-fitting lid and cook the onion, garlic and chillies, stirring frequently, for 5 minutes, or until softened. Add the kidney and cannellini beans and the chickpeas. Blend the tomato purée with a little of the stock in a jug and pour over the bean mixture, then add the remaining stock. Bring to the boil, then reduce the heat and simmer for 10–15 minutes.

Add the red pepper, tomatoes, broad beans, and pepper to taste and simmer for a further 15–20 minutes, or until all the vegetables are tender. Stir in the chopped coriander.

Serve the stew topped with spoonfuls of soured cream and garnished with chopped coriander and a pinch of paprika.

SERVES 4–6

2 tbsp olive oil

1 onion, chopped

2–4 garlic cloves, chopped

2 fresh red chillies, deseeded and sliced

225 g/8 oz canned kidney beans, drained and rinsed

225 g/8 oz canned cannellini beans, drained and rinsed

225 g/8 oz canned chickpeas, drained and rinsed

1 tbsp tomato purée

700–850 ml/$1^1/_4$–$1^1/_2$ pints vegetable stock

1 red pepper, deseeded and chopped

4 tomatoes, roughly chopped

175 g/6 oz frozen or shelled fresh broad beans, thawed if frozen

pepper

1 tbsp chopped fresh coriander, plus extra to garnish

soured cream, to serve

paprika, to garnish

Lentil & Rice Casserole

Place the lentils, rice and vegetable stock in a large flameproof casserole and cook over a low heat, stirring occasionally, for 20 minutes.

Add the leek, garlic, tomatoes and their can juice, ground cumin, chilli powder, garam masala, red pepper, broccoli, baby sweetcorn and French beans to the pan.

Bring the mixture to the boil, reduce the heat, cover and simmer for a further 10–15 minutes or until the vegetables are tender.

Add the shredded basil and season with salt and pepper to taste.

Garnish with fresh basil sprigs and serve immediately.

SERVES 4

225 g/8 oz red lentils

55 g/2 oz long-grain rice

1.2 litres/2 pints vegetable stock

1 leek, cut into chunks

3 garlic cloves, crushed

400 g/14 oz canned chopped
 tomatoes

1 tsp ground cumin

1 tsp chilli powder

1 tsp garam masala

1 red pepper, deseeded and sliced

100 g/3½ oz small broccoli florets

8 baby sweetcorn, halved lengthways

55 g/2 oz French beans, halved

1 tbsp shredded fresh basil

salt and pepper

fresh basil sprigs, to garnish

Cauliflower & Sweet Potato Curry

Heat the ghee in a large, heavy-based frying pan. Add the onions and Panch Phoran and cook over a low heat, stirring frequently, for 10 minutes, or until the onions are golden. Add the cauliflower, sweet potatoes and chillies and cook, stirring frequently, for 3 minutes.

Stir in the ginger paste, paprika, cumin, turmeric and chilli powder and cook, stirring constantly, for 3 minutes. Add the tomatoes and peas and stir in the yogurt and stock. Season with salt to taste, cover and simmer for 20 minutes, or until the vegetables are tender.

Sprinkle the garam masala over the curry, transfer to a warmed serving dish and serve immediately, garnished with fresh coriander sprigs.

SERVES 4

4 tbsp ghee or vegetable oil

2 onions, finely chopped

1 tsp Panch Phoran

1 cauliflower, broken into
 small florets

350 g/12 oz sweet potatoes, diced

2 fresh green chillies, deseeded and
 finely chopped

1 tsp ginger paste

2 tsp paprika

$1^1/_2$ tsp ground cumin

1 tsp ground turmeric

$^1/_2$ tsp chilli powder

3 tomatoes, quartered

225 g/8 oz fresh or frozen peas

3 tbsp natural yogurt

225 ml/8 fl oz vegetable stock or
 water

salt

1 tsp garam masala

fresh coriander sprigs, to garnish

Parmesan Cheese Risotto with Mushrooms

Heat the oil in a deep saucepan. Add the rice and cook over a low heat, stirring constantly, for 2–3 minutes, until the grains are thoroughly coated in oil and translucent.

Add the garlic, onion, celery and red pepper and cook, stirring frequently, for 5 minutes. Add the mushrooms and cook for 3–4 minutes. Stir in the oregano.

Gradually add the hot stock, a ladle at a time. Stir constantly and add more liquid as the rice absorbs each addition. Increase the heat to medium so that the liquid bubbles. Cook for 20 minutes, or until all the liquid is absorbed and the rice is creamy. Add the sun-dried tomatoes, if using, 5 minutes before the end of the cooking time and season to taste with salt and pepper.

Remove the risotto from the heat and stir in half the Parmesan until it melts. Transfer the risotto to warmed bowls. Top with the remaining cheese, garnish with flat-leaf parsley or bay leaves and serve immediately.

SERVES 6

2 tbsp olive oil or vegetable oil

225 g/8 oz risotto rice

2 garlic cloves, crushed

1 onion, chopped

2 celery sticks, chopped

1 red or green pepper, deseeded and chopped

225 g/8 oz mushrooms, thinly sliced

1 tbsp chopped fresh oregano or 1 tsp dried oregano

1 litre/$1^3/_4$ pints simmering vegetable stock

55 g /2 oz sun-dried tomatoes in olive oil, drained and chopped (optional)

salt and pepper

55 g/2 oz finely grated Parmesan cheese

fresh flat-leaf parsley sprigs or bay leaves, to garnish